Stephanie Lipka

Female Cunningness and Male Deceptionse
and Sensibility' and in Henry Fielding's 'T

C000130840

GRIN - Verlag für akademische Texte

Der GRIN Verlag mit Sitz in München hat sich seit der Gründung im Jahr 1998 auf die Veröffentlichung akademischer Texte spezialisiert.

Die Verlagswebseite www.grin.com ist für Studenten, Hochschullehrer und andere Akademiker die ideale Plattform, ihre Fachtexte, Studienarbeiten, Abschlussarbeiten oder Dissertationen einem breiten Publikum zu präsentieren.

Dokument Nr. V126046 aus dem GRIN Verlagsprogramm

Stephanie Lipka

Female Cunningness and Male Deception in Jane Austen's 'Northanger Abbey' and 'Sense and Sensibility' and in Henry Fielding's 'Tom Jones'

GRIN Verlag

Bibliografische Information der Deutschen Nationalbibliothek: Die Deutsche Bibliothek
verzeichnet diese Publikation in der Deutschen Nationalbibliografie; detaillierte bibliografische Daten sind im Internet über http://dnb.d-nb.de/ abrufbar.

1. Auflage 2001
Copyright © 2001 GRIN Verlag
http://www.grin.com/
Druck und Bindung: Books on Demand GmbH, Norderstedt Germany
ISBN 978-3-640-31808-7

Literaturwissenschaftliches Hauptseminar
Comedy and Burlesque in Henry Fielding and Jane Austen

Sommersemester 2001

Female Cunningness and Male Deception
in Jane Austen's *Northanger Abbey* and *Sense and Sensibility* and in Henry Fielding's *Tom Jones*

Stephanie Lipka

5. Fachsemester
Lehramt Sek. II/I
Englisch, Pädagogik

Table of Contents

Introduction   1

Part 1
Female Cunningness in Jane Austen's
Northanger Abbey and *Sense and Sensibility*   2

Male Deception in *Northanger Abbey* and
Sense and Sensibility   10

Part 2
Female Cunningness from a Male Point of View
Lady Bellaston in Henry Fielding's *Tom Jones*   14

Male Intrigues in *Tom Jones*   18

Conclusion   22

Literature   II

Introduction

When comparing Jane Austen's novels *Northanger Abbey* and *Sense and Sensibility* to Henry Fielding's *Tom Jones*, the reader's first observation will be that they do not have too much in common. Jane Austen tells romantic love stories. Henry Fielding mostly deals with sex. Jane Austen's main characters are women waiting for and suffering on behalf of a man. Henry Fielding describes male behaviour.

In this work, I want to take a closer look at the differences between the novels. Focussing on cunning and intrigue - how do the authors present their characters? In both *Northanger Abbey* and *Sense and Sensibility*, we come across women of relatively low social status who want to improve their lifestyle by marrying a wealthy man. We also come across men who turn out to be not what they seem: men that (in *Northanger Abbey*) lack responsibility or who (in *Sense and Sensibility*) are too responsible. In *Tom Jones*, we find two both evil and cunning characters one of whom is male. This work focusses on these characters' motives, actions and on the effects of these. Furthermore, it deals with the question whether their behaviour is judged by the authors.

Genre will not be focussed on, but the questions mentioned beforehand will be answered by a closer examination of style. A man thinks differently from a woman; he presents female and male characters in another way than a woman would and he expresses his thoughts in a different manner.

Starting from the topic of cunning and intrigue, the following pages will deal with the different perception and presentation of both female cunning and male deception in the novels - depending on the author's sex.

Part 1

Female Cunning in Jane Austen's
Northanger Abbey and *Sense and Sensibility*

In *Northanger Abbey* and in *Sense and Sensibility*, the reader is confronted with two kinds of female cunning employed for different reasons - but both aiming at defeating a possible rival in love. In *Northanger Abbey*, we come across Isabella Thorpe, a beautiful young woman of 21. Isabella is everything Catherine is not. She wants to have attention, is eager to get a man and has one great advantage over her inexperienced friend:

> "Their [Isabella's and Catherine's] conversation turned upon those subjects, of which the free discussion has generally much to do in perfecting a sudden intimacy between two young ladies; such as dress, balls, flirtations, and quizzes. Miss Thorpe, however, being four years older than Miss Morland, and at least four years better informed, had a very decided advantage in discussing such points; she could compare the balls of Bath with those of Tunbridge; its fashions with the fashions of London; could rectify the opinions of her new friend in many articles of tasteful attire; could discover a flirtation between any gentleman and lady who only smiled at each other; and point out a quiz through the thickness of a crowd."(NA, IV, 30)

From the beginning of their acquaintance, the reader is brought to the impression that the clever Isabella uses Catherine as a kind of negative. She instantly realizes that the young girl is plain and shy, the ideal friend at whose side she can sparkle and shine and be admired. Gabriela Castellanos describes her as "a fortune-hunting, shallow, hypocritical young lady"[1] pursuing only one genuine interest "in spite of her duplicity and mercenary spirit"[2]: men. Convinced of Catherine's brother James' wealth[3], Isabella seeks her friendship to lay hands on the desired object. Catherine does not see Isabella's intention although the Thorpes refer to James' stay at their home over christmas (NA, IV, 29). It was then that James met the charming and emancipated Isabella and fell in love with her and Isabella formed her idea of marrying him and even drops hints of her

---

[1] Castellanos, Gabriela, *Laughter, War and Feminism. Elements of Carnival in Three of Jane Austen's Novels*, New York: 1994, 86.
[2] ibd., 87.
[3] ibd., 91. "In the present case, the mask torn away reveals the deepest motive behind Isabella's deception, greed. Isabella, the reader will later find, set out to conquer James' affection because she was deceived as to the extent of his father's wealth."

intention to Catherine who does not understand them. In chapter V already, Isabella speaks of her liking for clergymen (NA, V, 33) one of whom is James Morland and gives a little sigh. But Catherine does not ask for the cause of this sigh. She does not see through Isabella's allusions and is sure that Isabella's only interest is to help her get Mr Tilney's attention. Although she has only met him once, Catherine believes Mr Tilney to be the love of her life, and, of course, she thinks a lot about him - as any young girl would who has just experienced her first ball, her first dance and her first conversation with a witty and handsome young man. Isabella even enforces these reflections and tells Catherine to put all her zeal into catching her man. In chapter VI, she assures Catherine that her

> "feelings are easily understood. Where the heart is really attached, I know very well how little one can be pleased with the attention of any body else. Every thing[sic] is so insipid, so uninteresting, that does not relate to the beloved object! I can perfectly comprehend your feelings!" (NA, VI, 38),

yet it is not Catherine's fancied man she is referring to but her own. And when Catherine opposes her with her natural logic saying that she might never meet Mr Tilney again, Isabella's character starts to show for she presses Catherine not to give up the man but to act and face him. She in a way instructs Catherine to copy her feminine ways and treat men with coolness and an opposing spirit:

> "I make it a rule never to mind what they (men) say. They are very often amazingly impertinent if you do not treat them with spirit, and make them keep their distance." (NA, VI, 38)

Catherine is impressed with this behaviour, but she does not realize that Isabella's feminism is artificial. It is only a "pose, for Isabella's first object is to make males worship her. Men are, therefore, the center of her life, as surely as they would be if she acted submissively toward them"[4]. We can, thus, say that Isabella blinds Catherine with a strength of character she does not possess and tricks her into thinking of her as an independent and adorable person. Isabella's intention is, of course, Catherine's positive judgment when talking to James.

---

[4] Castellanos, Gabriela, *Laughter, War and Feminism. Elements of Carnival in Three of Jane Austen's Novels*, New York: 1994, 91.

Her last attempt to hint at a match between herself and James is Isabella's comparison
of tastes in men:

> "I have not forgot your description of Mr Tilney; - 'a brown skin, with dark eyes,
> and rather dark hair.' - Well, my taste is different. I prefer light eyes, and as to
> complexion - do you know - I like a sallow better than any other. You must not betray me,
> if you should ever meet with one of your acquaintance answering that description."
> "Betray you! - What do you mean?"
> "Nay, do not distress me. I believe I have said too much. Let us drop the subject." (NA, VI, 39)

Obviously, Catherine does not think of Isabella's talking of James, and so -when
reunited with James at Bath- Isabella charms him directly, neglecting her friend
Catherine. James is easily impressed and praises Isabella as "thoroughly unaffected and
amiable" (NA, VII, 46), and in the following, Isabella and James seldom separate,
leaving Catherine to herself at balls (as in NA,VIII, 48). Yet, there is Isabella's boastful
brother John Thorpe keeping Catherine company and trying to court her. But his
manners are not so refined as Isabella's, and he directly asks about Catherine's property,
alluding to Catherine's friend Mr Allen's having no children of his own and being her
godfather, thus to her being one of his heirs (NA, IX, 57-58). So John Thorpe's
intention becomes obvious right from the start. Like his sister, he wants to marry
wealthy; knowing about Catherine's clumsiness, he thinks of her as of an easy prey. But
Catherine does not like him (NA, VII, 46) and only accepts his company because he is
Isabella's brother and James' friend.

Isabella's and John's cunning shows -at least to the reader- when they spoil a set of
Catherine's walks with the Tilneys (NA, XI, 77-78; XIII, 87-90). Catherine begins to
feel that there is something wrong with the way she is treated by Isabella, yet she is not
sure about her friend's actions. She only starts to wonder at remarks such as "And did
Isabella never change her mind before?" (pronounced by Mr Tilney when Isabella
dances with his brother while James Morland is out of town, NA, XVI, 118) and "Is it
my brother's attentions to Miss Thorpe, or Miss Thorpe's admission of them, that gives
[James] the pain?" (also pronounced by Mr Tilney when Catherine confronts him with
his brother's courting Isabella, NA, IXX, 132-133), but nevertheless, she trusts her
friend. It is only when James writes to her to tell her of Isabella's not marrying him

(NA, XXV, 175-176), that Catherine understands Isabella's wrongs, and when Isabella writes to her (NA, XXVII, 188-189) because she wants to get back together with James that she sees through Isabella's character. She understands the letter's "inconsistencies, contradictions, and falsehood" and thinks: "She must think me an idiot, or she could not have written so; but perhaps this has served to make her character better known to me than mine is to her. I see what she has been about. She is a vain coquette, and her tricks have not answered" (NA, XXVII, 190).

From a female point of view, one can say that Isabella's behaviour is understandable though morally not acceptable. But we have to keep in mind that by the time *Northanger Abbey* was finished, 1803, and in the period before[5], from a woman's point of view, everything depended on society, on the seeing and being seen, on presenting oneself most profitably and making a good match; as Rachel Trickett puts it, "Jane Austen records accurately the social distinctions and the status of her characters - the amount of their estate or the extent of their lack of it, their family background, their rise or fall in fortune"[6]. At a time when one's own or one's family's money played the most important role in match-making, it is perfectly normal to hide one's lack of it and to try to impress with one's advantages. Isabella Thorpe is neither rich nor remarkably educated[7], but she sets her aims high and does not avoid "improper, reckless or vulgar actions"[8] to reach them.

---

[5] Butler, Marilyn, Introduction. Writing 1798-1817, in: Jane Austen, *Northanger Abbey*, London: 1995, xiv: "*Northanger Abbey* is essentially a work of the late 1790s. [ ] each certain allusion to another text dates before 1800. The Gothic novels listed by Isabella at Bath (I, iii) as being currently the rage belong to the years 1794-9. The novels most closely used in the text [ ] include a number of works of the 1780s, some even earlier. [ ] Other leading cultural themes - the picturesque, gardening, estate management, the modernization of ancient buildings - are equally characteristic of the 1790s, and will perhaps appear specific to that decade, when some of the detail is more closely examined."

[6] Trickett, Rachel, Manners and Society, in: David Grey (ed.), *The Jane Austen Handbook*, London: 1986, 297.

[7] see 5, xxxv-xxxvii: Her ignorance of or indifference towards manners in society makes Isabella "the self-appointed Mistress of Ceremonies of the quartet of young Morlands and Thorpes, which she rules by whim and dictat". She boasts and thinks she can act as she pleases. Being in the company of mostly richer people, Isabella tries to invent and dictate new styles ("[at] most this is a new hat"), but she "has to achieve stylishness through cheap accessories" because she cannot afford a large wardrobe full of different dresses. As for education, "[t]hough she instantly turns Catherine into a fan of Mrs Radcliffe, Isabella is not much of a reader herself. Books serve as one of her conversational gambits". "Isabella spreads the news about the latest commodities". "Her news items are really news flashes [ ]: what is in a shop window, or playing at the theatre, or who is contemplating adultery with whom". Isabella merely uses literature to underline her own interests or to feign knowledge or world-wiseness.

[8] ibd., xxxvii.

As for cunning, we have to say that Isabella is a self-centered person whose only interest is moving up the social ladder; and though Catherine does not understand Isabella's intentions, she gives indirect hints as to her desire of marrying James Morland. However, she tricks herself when she tranfers her attention from James to Captain Tilney because he appears to be an even more promising partner. After the openly shown affection towards James, this behaviour must be called a social *faux-pas*, only worsened by her letter to Catherine in which she asks for understanding and pity. It remains unclear whether Isabella really regrets her behaviour towards James Morland or whether she just regrets having lost both admirers and thus being forced to restart her search. Equally uncertain is whether people like Isabella are able to feel love or affection for another person. She never thinks of marriage for love, but only calculates the benefits of it.

By making Isabella Catherine's friend and tutor, Jane Austen creates tension. She makes the reader aware of Isabella's recklessness and egoism and lets him/her think about possible consequences for and effects on the heroine. Isabella -strong, persistant and clever- is used as a figure of contrast, as Catherine is shy, non-imposing and appears a bit naive. By letting Isabella deceive Catherine, Austen also gives her character an instructive function. Catherine learns about life without being deeply hurt, and she understands that intrigue and egoism are no positive traits of character. That Jane Austen opposes the hypocrisy of people like Isabella as well, becomes obvious when Isabella loses her two admirers while Catherine -all innocence and unimpressiveness- finally gets the man of her dreams.

A similar scheme is used in *Sense and Sensibility*, published in 1811[9], where Lucy Steele tries to save her engagement to Edward Ferrars. As she is neither rich nor educated[10], her chances of meeting a promising husband are rather limited. She therefore takes her first chance and enters into an engagement with a young man

---

[9] In the preface to *Sense and Sensibility* (London: Penguin, 1994) we are told that the novel "was reworked twice in the fourteen years before its publication in 1811". Over a period of 15 years, an author's ideas might well have changed.

[10] Austen, Jane, *Sense and Sensibility*, London: Penguin, 1994, 123-124: "Lucy was naturally clever; [ ]but her powers had received no aid from education, she was ignorant and illiterate, and her deficiency of all mental improvement, her want of information in the most common particulars, could not be concealed from Miss Dashwood." Lucy is a person "who join[s] insincerity with ignorance".

at her father's school. Edward Ferrars lacks all possible ambition and wants to be a clergyman; but Lucy knows that he will be the heir of a considerable fortune. For the following four years, they stay engaged as Edward wants to settle in a parish before telling his parents about his future marriage. But Edward meets another woman, the intelligent and witty Elinor Dashwood, and begins to compare the two. Elinor does not know of Lucy's existence, but Edward tells his fiancée of Elinor - and Lucy does not lose a second to try and get the other woman out of her way (SS, XXII, 124-126). Lucy chooses Elinor as a confidante - already knowing that this will hurt her adversary. But Elinor remains calm and gives no hint as to her emotions.

Where Isabella in *Northanger Abbey* completely hides the object of her motive, Lucy does not hesitate to tell Elinor every detail of her love to Edward, always shooting meaningful or testing glances at her to get a reaction[11]. Lucy is direct, yet not honest with Elinor. After having told her about the engagement, she tries to get an utterance of hurt feelings from Elinor by emphasizing that she might have hurt her with her words (SS,. XXIV, 140) - adding implicitly that Edward could have no feelings for Elinor:

> "I am rather of a jealous temper, too, by nature, and from our different situation in life, from his being so much more in the world than me, and our continual separation, I was enough inclined for suspicion to have found out the truth in an instant, if there had been the slightest alteration in his behaviour to me when we met, or any lowness of spirits that I could not account for, or if he had talked more of one lady than another. [ ] I do not mean to say that I am particularly observant or quicksighted in general, but in such a case I am sure I could not be deceived." (SS, XXIV, 141-142)

Her second try is a false over-estimation of Elinor's judgment which is revealed by telling Elinor that -following her judgment alone, she would end her engagement (SS, XXIV, 144). But once again, Elinor cannot be tricked into any form of personal statement. Other than Catherine who does not see Isabella's cunning, Elinor proves more intelligent than Lucy. She realizes that -assuming Lucy's claims are true- she has no chance of breaking these two people's relationship up. She is proud and reasonable to see that an engagement is a serious bond while her acquaintance with Edward Ferrars is only a superficial -though emotional- one.

---

[11] Austen, Jane, *Sense and Sensibility*, London: Penguin, 1994, 130: "[W]iping her eyes", Lucy tells Elinor about her lonely hours without Edward. And she observes her conversational partner (SS, XXIV, 142).

Elinor does not try to fight windmills and accepts the facts she learns from Lucy. And this is the fatal mistake that Lucy makes. In contrast to Elinor, Lucy thinks herself invincible. She acts out of the pure conviction that Edward must keep his promise to her because this is what she wants and what she has been waiting for for years. Once again, it is the character's hypocrisy that brings the fall. Edward feels tied to her, and though he is ready to marry her, he does not love her. Had Lucy been more subtle, more compromising and enduring, she would have been successful. But it takes her a long time to learn what Elinor already knows (-namely that it is her egoism that brings her to keeping "a man to an engagement of which she seemed so thoroughly aware that he was weary", SS, XXIV, 145) and to write to Edward that she will be happy with his brother and she will not think ill of him (SS, XLIX, 358).

Jane Austen mostly criticizes the egoism and hypocrisy among women of her society. She describes their motives, which are money and men (providing the desired money), and puts them into contrast with personality and true feeling. It is never the materialistic girls that *win* in her novels, but the honest heroines. Isabella's cunning does not pay at all. In Lucy's case, Jane Austen offers at least a hint of personal improvement. Lucy finally understands that it would be wrong to marry a man who loves another woman (She says so in her letter, SS, XLIX, 358.), and so the altered Lucy is rewarded with another husband.

Jane Austen's ways of presenting female cunning are subtle. She identifies with her characters, strictly putting them into the fixed corset of her social code. The reader therefore can understand why Isabella and Lucy are so eager to get a rich husband and why they have to make use of tricks to reach it. Other than Catherine, who is honest and pleasingly quiet, Isabella is a shrill character without any striking features (apart from being shrill). Thus, she has to use tricks to gain Catherine's brother's and other men's attention. Lucy makes use of her cunning because there is the danger of losing her fiancé. When she starts her little war against Elinor, she only knows her opponent to be another woman. But when she meets Elinor, she realizes that the other is more intelligent and charming, too. This hurts her pride and she desperately tries to restore it by winning over Elinor.

As mentioned before, Jane Austen underlines the quietness of intrigue. Her characters do not spread ill news about other people. Austen's female characters act eye to eye. Their actions often contradict their speech. Isabella's intention when telling Catherine not to mention her liking for a certain type of man to her family (NA, VI, 39), for example, is just that. She wants Catherine to tell her brother. Same with Lucy. When she confides in Elinor, she only waits for the other's reaction. She would never listen to any of Elinor's advices nor is she ignorant of Elinor's knowing Edward (SS, XXIV, 141; 144) - for this is her only reason for seeing Elinor.

Jane Austen perfectly shows that, with her female characters, one has to read between the lines. She proves to be a good observer of her sex, and, whether or not speaking out of experience, Jane Austen concludes that female cunning is not what a man desires in a woman.

Male Deception in *Northanger Abbey* and *Sense and Sensibility*

When there are female characters in Jane Austen's novels who make use of their cunning, there are male characters who pretend to be what they are not as well.

In *Northanger Abbey*, there is only one male who can be called a deceiver: Captain Frederick Tilney, "who can match and excell Isabella at her own game. Thus we see him parrying with Isabella in the most fashionable language of coquetry (cf. NA, 147), playing the gallant to Isabella's damsel"[12]. At a ball, he dances with Isabella, though she has earlier refused to dance because James Morland is not at the ball. As for Captain Tilney's motive, one can say that he is attracted by Isabella's beauty (NA, XVI, 119). His intention is to have fun at the ball, and after having consulted Henry Tilney on the subject of Catherine and Isabella (and after Henry's certainly having informed him about Isabella's character), he asks her - and Isabella is only too willing to dance (NA, XVI, 117-120). When Catherine asks Henry Tilney for an explanation of his brother's behaviour, Tilney only says that he has informed his brother of Isabella's engagement to James Morland, but that Captain Tilney is a "lively, and perhaps sometimes a thoughtless young man" (NA, IXX, 133).

When Isabella breaks up her engagement and James Morland writes to Catherine that Isabella is going to marry Captain Tilney instead, the Tilneys are much surprised and cannot understand why he would choose a woman of no fortune who is -to make things worse- "an unprincipled one" (NA, XXV, 178). Eleanor Tilney tells Catherine that the captain is a proud man "who found no woman good enough to be loved" (NA, XXV, 179) - and now he seems to have been trapped by Isabella. But as Isabella writes in her letter, the captain has gone back to sea again without even telling her goodbye (NA, XXVII, 188-189).

The character of Captain Tilney is used by Jane Austen as a sort of *emergency brake* to prevent James Morland from marrying false Isabella. Yet, the deceiver who deceives the deceiver is a "figure beyond moral judgment"[13]. Captain Tilney is a young man with principles, but ready to have fun when going out. He appears to come between Isabella

---

[12] Castellanos, Gabriela, *Laughter, War and Feminism. Elements of Carnival in Three of Jane Austen's Novels*, New York: 1994, 93.
[13] ibd.

and James Morland and disappears before he could be married by Isabella. His conduct may be judged ill by society, yet - in the great scheme of things - he does no harm. His task is only to court Isabella; and the fact that he neither speaks nor takes part in family trips with his sister and brother shows that his character is not an important one. Jane Austen does not characterize his manner or mind, but he is defined by his and Isabella's improper conduct.

In *Sense and Sensibility*, the case is different. In this novel, we come across two male deceivers, both doing harm but bringing about a certain maturation in the female characters who are deceived. We have, however, to distinguish between the two deceivers. Edward Ferrars is not of the same kind as Willoughby. Where Edward does not deceive Elinor as far as his feelings for her are concerned, he does deceive her by making her believe that there could be a match between them. It has to be admitted, though, that Edward possesses a certain constancy as he does not give up his engagement of four years for a new love he has known for several months. Willoughby, on the other hand, is available - but he does not have any strong feelings for Marianne. This shows when he marries a rich woman instead. There, he only thinks of his personal benefit. Had he really loved Marianne, he would have settled on a small income.

Jane Austen presents two different kinds of deception. In the first case, almost no harm is done because -even if he has concealed his engagement- Edward really loves Elinor, and she knows that. In the second case, Marianne is driven to a nervous breakdown and is full of despair, while Willoughby hard-heartedly marries another woman. It may well be that Jane Austen attempts to criticize her society by showing that formality and property are the engines moving society, and not true love, trust and friendship[14]- the virtues that dominate her novels. Her society is a patriarchal one; and this is reflected in the power men have over women. While they come and go and thus embody mobility, the women stay indoors waiting for men to provide them with news and gossip.

It must, however, be mentioned that neither Edward nor Willoughby intend to do harm. At least Edward is not looking for willing victims to abuse. In Willoughby's case, one

---

[14] Perkins, Morland, *Reshaping the Sexes in Sense and Sensibility*, Charlottesville, London: 1998, 106-107.

has to remember that he has already ruined the future prospects of Colonel Brandon's protégée Eliza by impregnating her (SS, XXXI, 202-204). One cannot be entirely sure of him having not done the same to Marianne, but he himself tells Elinor that he truly feels for Marianne and asks for forgiveness (SS, XLIV, 310-325). He describes his necessity of making love to Miss Grey that resulted from his aunt's disapproval of a possible match with poor Marianne - and Elinor forgives him[15]. And at the end of the novel, Austen makes clear that Willoughby -married to Miss Grey- still thinks of Marianne (SS, L, 373).

As Perkins points out, the reader cannot call in question Willoughby's confession at this point[16]. As he is a man who likes to spend lots of money on his amusement, he has to make a decision: whether to marry the poor Marianne or to find a rich woman with whom he could be more or less equally happy. Perkins speaks of Willoughby's "internal conflict and [ ] divided self"[17] that make him a better person than one would think him to be at first sight. The same works for Edward who "refus[es] to break with Lucy"[18] although he loves Elinor. Jane Austen reflects on her male characters' deceptions and tries to give a psychological explanation for them. In both cases, she underlines that both men have too much freedom. While Willoughby is a gentleman who does not have to work for a living[19], Edward is on his way of becoming a clergyman, though he does not seem to do anything but wait for the right moment to tell his family about his engagement with Lucy. The difference between the two men is that Willoughby admits to being a "rascal" (SS, XLIV, 317), but he does not see why. He only sees the necessity in marrying a wealthy woman. Edward, on the other hand, reflects upon his situation and offers the explanation that he has too much liberty. The lack of work and the lack of an aim in his life are the causes of his idleness (SS, XLIX, 355) which has led him to his engagement. He admits having got engaged because he had nothing else to do.

---

[15] Austen, Jane, *Sense and Sensibility*, London: Penguin: 1994, 323. Elinor chooses the words: "You have proved yourself, on the whole, less faulty than I had believed you. You have proved your heart less wicked, much less wicked."
[16] Perkins, Morland, *Reshaping the Sexes in Sense and Sensibility*, Charlottesville, London: 1998, 113.
[17] ibd., 118-119.
[18] ibd.
[19] ibd., 126.

At second thought, he calls this engagement a "foolish" idea (SS, XLIX, 355).

> "All too often, in Austen's view, lack of a profession brings with it lack of purpose, vacant time, and either an income demoralizingly dependent on personal ties or, if the young man with no profession is independent, egotism, lack of discipline, extravagance, debt, and finally in both cases: the absence of true freedom in some major choices. In this novel an appropriate share of these afflictions directly exerts an oppressive force on the early life of Edward and on the entire life of Willoughby."[20]

In a way, Jane Austen uses this lack of employment as some kind of social criticism as well. She does not judge the men's behaviour and place herself on the women's side, but she reflects on the causes of it. This analyzing is typical in a woman. When she does not understand a man's behaviour, she tries to put herself in his place and wants to find out what goes on in his mind, while a man might not think about anything at all. Women are exact observers of human behaviour, but they tend to over-interpret male behaviour because to them it is equal to the female[21].

As a female writer, Jane Austen describes her male characters from a female point of view, which makes them more sympathetic than they would appear if Jane Austen only stated their actions. In giving the female reader an insight into (what she regards as)the male psyche, her characters get a notion of reality that is not real. And her characters are amiable or at least tolerable, and their thoughts and actions understandable - because they are fictitious men based on a woman's thoughts.

---

[20] Perkins, Morland, *Reshaping the Sexes in Sense and Sensibility*, Charlottesville, London: 1998, 124-125.
[21] as illustrated in Pease, Allan and Barbara, *Warum Männer nicht zuhören und Frauen schlecht einparken. Ganz natürliche Erklärungen für eigentlich unerklärliche Schwächen*, München: 2001, 201.

Part 2

Female Cunning from a Male Point of View
Lady Bellaston in Henry Fielding's *Tom Jones*

In Henry Fielding's *Tom Jones*, we come across a character called Lady Bellaston who - once she has started a brief affair with the hero - is very much interested in the future continuation of it. But her cousin and guest to her house Sophia turns out to be Tom Jones' love and is in love with him as well.

Unlike Jane Austen, Henry Fielding instantly calls a spade a spade and opens Lady Bellaston's intrigue with the words:

> "[U]nder all the smiles which she bore in her countenance, (Lady Bellaston)concealed much indignation against Sophia; and as she plainly saw, that this young lady stood between her and the full indulgence of her desires, she resolved to get rid of her by some means or other." (TJ, XV, 2, 648)

Lady Bellaston aims at Sophia's destruction, and as she herself is an old and cunning woman -so rich that she can imagine herself out of the bounds of law- she would do anything to please her hurt pride. She intends to prove herself that her cleverness and influence can make her superior to any other person. Instead of accepting Tom's leaving her, she wants to destroy his beloved Sophia by putting him into as bad a light as possible.

Bellaston's first step is the introduction of another admirer to Sophia. Lord Fellamar likes the girl very much, and so Lady Bellaston encourages his courting Sophia, at the same time informing the lord of his most dangerous rival: Tom Jones, "a beggar, a bastard, a foundling, a fellow in meaner circumstances than one of your lordship's footmen"(TJ, XV, 2, 651). Though Lady Bellaston generally appears as a sexually aggressive character, in convincing the lord of her schemes, she uses a certain subtlety[22] of behaviour. She assures the lord of her being only a weak woman who is at her wit's end (TJ, XV, 2, 651) and of his being the only one who can prevent Sophia from great

---

[22] Spacks, Patricia Meyer, *Desire and Truth*, Chicago: 1990, 61. Lady Bellaston's aggressive behaviour shows when she writes a number of letters to her lover Tom commanding him to come to her immediately (TJ, XV, 9, 676) or when she goes to see him (TJ, XIV, 2, 612-615) and places herself in a rather immoral position.

misery, thus clothing her evil plan in a pleasing outfit. To prove Sophia's love to Tom, Lady Bellaston has somebody tell her that Tom has been killed, and from the girl's emotional reaction, Lord Fellamar can deduce her strong affection for him. And although Sophia begs Lady Bellaston not to leave her alone with "that odious lord" (TJ, XV, 3, 655), the lady sends him into her room. The lord does not approve of this inappropriate intrusion, but Lady Bellaston laughs at him and tells him that it is every woman's desire to be raped[23] . Now, there may be two possible explanations for her telling him such things: It may be pure hatred against Sophia and her sick desire of making the girl miserable. But it may as well be a way of expressing her own desires. As an experienced, yet unmarried, woman, she might remember her own sexual contacts and feel a sad memorabilia towards those lovers who have given her the greatest pleasure[24]. Lady Bellaston, however, is fully conscious of Sophia's resistance - so that she sends Sophia's maid into another part of the house (TJ, XV, 3, 654) and dismisses her own servants (TJ, XV, 5, 659). Luckily, Sophia is saved from rape by the arrival of her angry father.

But Lady Bellaston is not yet satisfied. As soon as Sophia is out of the house, the lady writes to Tom to renew their sexual relationship. But Tom has learned, too. With the help of his friend Nightingale, he has come to see through the net of Lady Bellaston's ill-use of power (consisting of "money, social authority and erotic energy"[25]) and he can use it to get rid of her. Just as Nightingale has predicted to Tom, Lady Bellaston reacts very angrily to his marriage-proposal (TJ, XV, 9, 679) because she "understands [it] as a threat to her autonomy and an effort to gain possession of her wealth"(TJ, XV, 9, 679). She knows that her game is up and that Tom has leaned to play it, and this gives her pride an even greater pang than does his love for Sophia.

---

[23] Fielding, Henry, *Tom Jones*, London: Penguin, 1985, 656. Lady Bellaston mocks the lord by asking him whether he was "frighted by the word *rape*". Then, she enumerates cases of rape, ending sarcastically that "they made tolerable good wives afterwards". The lord has his doubts, but Lady Bellaston's argument that "any woman in England would [ ] laugh at [him]" and his prudery, convinces him that she as a woman must know and can tell him best what to do to win Sophia's body and soul.
[24] Belsey, Catherine, *Desire. Love Stories in Western Culture*, Oxford: 1994, 17-29. Belsey defines desire as a longing for over-powering and satisfaction, and she underlines that women do desire a pure physical experience, and therefore a dominant man who nearly rapes the woman but who is so feeling and knowing that he would never really hurt her. In literature -especially in kitchen-sink literature- orgasms are used as climaxes, or rather highlights, in the actions.

Lady Bellaston's revenge is her making use of her influence over Lord Fellamar once more and of trying to persuade him into sending Tom into naval service (TJ, XVI, 8, 718). Her second step is to give Tom's marriage-proposal to Mrs Western. The latter is shocked and surprised that Tom should propose to the lady and tries to inquire into this affair, but Lady Bellaston does not specify her relationship with Tom and even lies about their intimacy("`[ ] how did you use the fellow?´ returned Mrs Western. `Not as a husband,´ said the lady", TJ, XVI, 8, 719).

Fielding then provides his readership with an explanation of Lady Bellaston's behaviour:

> "But perhaps the reader may wonder why Lady Bellaston, who in her heart hated Sophia, should be so desirous of promoting a match (namely the wealthy Lord Fellamar), which was so much to the interest of the young lady. Now, I would desire such readers to look carefully into human nature, page almost the last, and there he will find in scarce legible characters, that [ ] a woman who hath once been pleased with the possession of a man, will go above half way to the devil, to prevent any other woman from enjoying the same." (TJ, XVI, 8, 719-720)

In contrast with Jane Austen's implicit explanations of female behaviour, Fielding puts his finger on it. He does not only describe what Lady Bellaston does, but he comments on her actions and admits to be on Sophia's side[26]. Just like Isabella and Lucy in Jane Austen's novels, Lady Bellaston is egoistic and, like Lucy, she tries to keep another woman away from her lover by all means. But in Austen's novels, these means are restricted to subtle eye-contact or implied meannesses. No real harm to a person's body or reputation is done. It is the mind that suffers. In *Tom Jones*, it is both body and mind. Lady Bellaston can be called a ruthless person without any regard for other people. All she wants is her private revenge and satisfaction; and instead of leaving her lover to Sophia -as Lucy leaves Edward Ferrars to Elinor when she has found another man- Lady Bellaston claws to him and wants to demonstrate her influence.

The other character in *Tom Jones* who uses her female cunning in face of a man is Harriet Fitzpatrick who ran away from her family to be married by an Irishman for her money and who is now running away from him (TJ, XI, 4-7).

---

[25] Spacks, Patricia Meyer, *Desire and Truth*, Chicago: 1990, 81.
[26] This becomes obvious in constantly referring to Sophia as "poor" (as in TJ, XV, 5, 659) and of speaking about her "destruction" (TJ, XV, 4, 657).

Mrs Fitzpatrick's anger can be explained by her husband's having betrayed her; and her resolution to leave him is taken when she finds a letter addressed to him revealing that he would have married either her or her aunt, but that he preferred her "on account of her ready money" (TJ, XI, 5, 480). But she stays with him nevertheless, has to move to Ireland with him and ends up a prisoner in his manor. Her husband having spent most of her money learns that she has kept some for herself and wants her to sign a paper giving him the authority of making use of it. Here, however, Mrs Fitzpatrick proves to be a clever woman - and with a friend's help, she is able to get out of her prison and back to England. This peer is not only described as an "intimate acquaintance", but also as a "very particular friend" (TJ, XI, 8, 498), leaving the degree of their intimacy to the readers' imagination. As Mrs Fitzpatrick is staying at the peer's house in London, they cannot be other than lovers. Even Sophia concludes this from the peer's behaviour in chapter 10 and decides to move to Lady Bellaston's house.

In Mrs Fitzpatrick's case, her female cunning is understandable. She uses the peer to get away from her mean husband and to protect her property. She does not use any intrigues and does not behave in any evil way towards other characters. She only tries to save herself and what is left of her money from her husband.[27]

As for the little hints in behaviour such as looks or gestures, one can say, that Fielding does not go into these details of non-verbal communication. His two cunning females are described from his male point of view - and this point of view is different from a female one. Women do not have to call a spade a spade, they do not stare, but they perceive things and actions in passing. Their means of perception are much less obvious than the male ones. That is why Fielding expresses directly what he wants to say, while Jane Austen as a female writer makes much use of indirect characterization, by letting her characters' bodies talk.

---

[27] Fielding, Henry, *Tom Jones*, London: Penguin, 1985, 505. Mrs Fitzpatrick seeks male protection.

18

Male Intrigues in *Tom Jones*

The main male villain in *Tom Jones* is Master Blifil who is jealous of his older brother. But not only has Tom had more time to gain people's friendship, he also is a foundling. This makes Blifil Jr. angry because he feels that the other child is more appreciated than he is. His behaviour can be explained by his childhood and the way his parents treated each other[28]. His father was a greedy captain who had married Miss Allworthy for her wealth and who already disliked Tom Jones because the foundling seemed to cross his plans of inheriting Allworthy's property (TJ, II, 2 and II, 8). This greed and the constant quarrel between his parents (TJ, II, 7) must have poisoned young Blifil's character; and when Bridget Blifil's affection finally turns from him (as her own son) to Tom (TJ, III, 6), Blifil becomes really jealous. He starts to insult Tom by calling him names (TJ, III, 4, 101) and uses Tom's little secrets -like killing birds with the gamekeeper- against him (TJ, III, 4). In revealing these, Blifil becomes a master who does not blackmail his brother but who is so cunning that he leaves hints of Tom's behaviour:

> "(Tom) was no sooner pardoned for selling [his] horse (to help the gamekeeper's family with the money), than he was discovered to have some time before sold a fine Bible which Mr Allworthy gave him, the money arising from which sale he had disposed in the same manner. This Bible Master Blifil had purchased, tho' he had already such another of his own [ ]. Some people have been noted to be able to read in no book but their own. On the contrary, from the time when Master Blifil was first possessed of this Bible, he never used any other. Nay, he was seen reading in it much oftener than he had before been in his own. Now, as he frequently asked Thwackum to explain difficult passages to him, that gentleman unfortunately took notice of Tom's name, which was written in many parts of the book. This brought on an enquiry, which obliged Master Blifil to discover the whole matter." (TJ, III, 9, 114-115)

Although Fielding does not explicitly say so, it becomes obvious that Blifil Jr. acts out of pure ill-will towards Tom. He just waits for his name to be discovered, so that he does not appear as the evil brother denouncing Tom but as the victim who is interviewed on this point and has to give Tom away. Yet, his mother does not think him

---

[28] Hafner, Dieter, *Tom Jones. Fieldings Roman und Osbornes Drehbuch. Untersuchungen zu einem Medienwechsel*, Bern: 1981, 122: "das von schwelenden Konflikten vergiftete Familienmilieu [ ], worin Fielding Tom und Blifil aufwachsen läßt: [ ] Man braucht nicht Psychologe zu sein, um hier Wurzeln der Rivalität zwischen Master Blifil und Tom Jones, den Bridget (Blifil) insgeheim bevorzugt, erkennen zu können."

as innocent as he presents himself. She insists on her opinion that there is "no difference between the buyer and the seller" (TJ, III, 9, 115).

The next accident happens when the two brothers have made the acquaintance of Sophia Western and Tom has given the girl a caged bird. Blifil -once more- is jealous because he sees that Sophia admires the wild and funny Tom but does not care about him at all (TJ, IV, 3, 125). He frees the bird and tries to explain that he had pity for the bird. Tom, on the other hand, tries to catch the bird because he sees Sophia crying for the lost animal[29]. Again, Blifil has no success with his action. The fathers are pleased with Tom's trying to catch the bird, not with his deed of freeing it (TJ, IV, 4, 127-129).

Up to this point, Fielding has not uttered any doubts as to Blifil's honest character, and there are no hints in the text for Blifil's jealousy. His explanations are not put into doubt but left to the reader's interpretation. In the following chapter, Fielding concludes from these interpretations that Blifil is a self-centered idle person[30]. Therefore, he hides from his sick uncle the letter he receives from his dying mother (TJ, V, 7 and 8, 196-199) in which she admits being Tom's mother, too. Blifil knows that Tom, being older, would be the proper heir of Allworthy's fortune, a fact which does not please him at all. To be really safe from Tom's interference, he has to get rid of him, so he repeats every mistake Tom has made while he was ill, to Allworthy (TJ, VI, 10, 250) who throws Tom out of his house immediately (TJ, VI, 11 and 12, 252-253). At the same time, Blifil grabs his chance of marrying the fortune of Sophia whose hand her father proposes to him. Upon this point, Fielding expresses his character's motives explicitly:

> "The charms of Sophia had not made the least impression on Blifil; not that his heart was pre-engaged; neither was he totally insensible of beauty,or had any aversion to women; but his appetites were, by nature, so moderate, that he was easily able, by philosophy or by study, or by some other method, to subdue them; and as to that passion which we have treated of in the first chapter of this book (which is love), he had not the least tincture of it in his whole composition. But tho' he was so entirely free from that mixed passion, of which we there treated, and of which the virtues and beauty of Sophia formed so notable an object; yet was he altogether as well furnished with some other passions, that promised themselves very full gratification in the young lady's fortune. Such were avarice and ambition" (TJ, VI, 4, 229).

---

[29] Harrison, Bernard, *Henry Fielding's Tom Jones. The Novelist as Moral Philosopher*, London: 1975, 28-29. "Blifil's humanitarianism is oddly limited in its objects. He *says* he feels for the bird what his subsequent utterance makes it quite clear that he does *not* feel for Sophia in her loss."
[30] Fielding, Henry, *Tom Jones*, London: Penguin, 1985, 130: "Master Blifil, tho' a prudent, discreet, sober, young gentleman, was, at the same time, strongly attached to the interest only of one single person; and who that single person was, the reader will be able to divine without any assistance of ours."

20

Furthermore, Blifil turns out to be a pervert who -because he is so utterly hated by Sophia- sees pleasure in having her be forced into marrying him. Fielding here offers an insight into Blifil's character:

> "Tho' Mr Blifil was not of the complexion of Jones, nor ready to eat every woman he saw, yet he was far from being destitute of that appetite which is said to be the common property of all animals. [ ] Now the agonies which affected the mind of Sophia rather augmented than impaired her beauty; for her tears added brightness to her eyes, and her breasts rose higher with her sighs. Indeed no one hath seen beauty in its highest lustre, who hath never seen it in distress. Blifil therefore looked on this human ortolan with desire than when he had viewed her last; nor was his desire at all lessened by the aversion which he discovered in her to himself. On the contrary, this served rather to heighten the pleasure he proposed in rifling her charms, as it added triumph to lust; nay, he had some further views, from obtaining the absolute possession of her person, which we detest too much even to mention; and revenge itself was not without its share in the gratifications which he promised himself." (TJ, VII, 6, 280)

Having shown how deeply rotten Blifil's spirit is[31], Fielding sums up Blifil's plans for deceiving Allworthy and Sophia's father (TJ, VII, 6, 281). But Sophia runs away to get away from Blifil and to find Tom. Therefore, Blifil's last straw is the attempt to have Tom hanged for murder (TJ, XVI, 10 and XVII, 2, 732-733). However, he does not succeed, and all his intrigues are revealed in the last book (TJ, XVIII, 8, 793 and chapters 10-12).

As for Blifil's motive, the secondary texts offer several explanations. In Reilly[32], we get an interpretation based on the Christian religion:

> "Blifil, bad from birth, twisted in mind and nature, is incapable of a good action; what seems like one in such a man is pure illusion - it *must* be perverted at its root. [ ] What a man *is* must color what he does; the wicked soul can perform only wicked acts. How can a bad tree bear good fruit? All these acts -freeing a bird, telling the truth, courting a woman- may be good in themselves [ ]. Everything depends on the how and the why of its doing. [ ] His heart *is* corrupt, his nature vicious."[33]

Assuming that Blifil is born evil, Reilly's text deals with the biblical figure of the Pharisee[34], the "hypocrite, fraud, pious dissembler, someone whose virtue is a pose, an

---

[31] Hafner, Dieter, *Tom Jones. Fieldings Roman und Osbornes Drehbuch. Untersuchungen zu einem Medienwechsel*, Bern: 1981, 121. Hafner puts it this way: "Das Perverseste an Blifils Liebeswerben ist im Roman, daß nicht nur sein Wunschobjekt ihn, sondern daß er selbst es immer mehr haßt".
[32] Reilly, Patrick, *Tom Jones. Adventure and Providence*, Boston: 1991, 27-61.
[33] ibd., 44-45.
[34] ibd., 36.

act, a performance; who deceives others, but knows himself"[35]. To his mind, Blifil must be called such an impostor, and thus, there is no way of ever altering Blifil's character. A liar will always lie to hide his faults, is what Reilly critisizes most, and he compares the liar to the sinner who is honest[36]. A sinner realizes that he makes mistakes while a liar deceives both the others and himself.[37]

Fielding uses the character of Blifil as a negative to Tom's. Though both men deceive (Tom must think to have fathered Molly's child, yet he is ready to leave her to her fate. He furthermore pretends to be innocent, yet he juggles with several lovers not thinking about Sophia's feelings.), Tom seems to get into situations which force him to lie, while Blifil is the evil spirit producing these situations. And though he is right in revealing *sins*, his means are wicked and his motives egoistic. One can say that in Blifil's case, honesty conceals wickedness. His intrigues are led by the motive of greed and jealousy the latter of which is understandable with regard to his youth[38]. He does not need to marry a wealthy woman, and neither does he have to destroy Tom's future plans, yet he tries to. At some passages in the novel, Fielding tries to explain Blifil's actions, yet a psychological background or detailed chain of Blifil's thoughts are missing. Other than Jane Austen presents her male deceivers in *Sense and Sensibility*, Fielding as a man merely judges immoral behaviour, but he does not try to explain it. He stays with the facts and lets his readership interpret Blifil's actions.

---

[35] Reilly, Patrick, *Tom Jones. Adventure and Providence*, Boston: 1991, 28.
[36] ibd., 27, 40.
[37] ibd., 28. "Deception" is found in the liar's behaviour towards others, the "self-deception" is the self-pity following the revelation of his lies and leading to new ones. The liar tries to appear in a most advantageous light thinking himself more cunning than everybody else; he is thus a hypocrite.

22

Conclusion

When comparing Jane Austen's way of presenting her characters to the way Fielding presents his, one becomes aware of the difference between female and male authors. Leaving aside the fact that Austen's novels have been written about fifty years after *Tom Jones* (1746-1748), and the English society may have had essentially changed in the course of those fifty years, there are, though, ways of dealing with intrigues that root in the sexes.

Jane Austen's style is much more subtle[39]. Her female characters appear passive - according to their social code waiting for a man- busily concealing their feelings until the man of their dreams comes to marry them. This works for Elinor in *Sense and Sensibility* as well as for Catherine in *Northanger Abbey*. Active women like Lucy or Isabella are not the novels' heroines. Their role is a didactic one showing that intrigues and ill-used cunning are not the proper means to be employed by a woman. To Jane Austen, moral conduct is most essential if one wants to raise high in society. And there is another difference to *Tom Jones* where the female main characters do not aspire to a higher social rank. Other than Austen's female characters, Sophia and Lady Bellaston are already women of society. Lady Bellaston can afford to do as she pleases and plays with her lovers, and Sophia's running away from home and refusing to obey her father's wishes also shows a certain willpower of her own. It is Blifil, a man, who wants money to improve his way of living. Other than in Jane Austen's novels, Blifil is said to be evil - thus, all his actions lead to something evil as well. Jane Austen's characters are backed up with much more psychology. Edward Ferrars' behaviour is explained with the innocense of youth and the lack of employment, Willoughby's with his lifestyle and too much freedom. The male characters' actions are reflected upon by the female ones. Elinor's thoughts have already made the reader acquainted with the reasons for the men's behaviour before they come and tell her (and the reader). These reasons are understandable for female readers because Jane Austen presents her female point of

---

[38] see 28.

view via that of Catherine or Elinor. From that point of view, every action has a reason and follows a certain logic.

Fielding, as a male writer, does not think about socially imposed reasons. To him, a person's character is either good or bad - and this character leads to all the person's actions. Jane Austen relates inner life and outer appearence or action, while to Fielding, the second are obvious.[40]He does not go into his characters' thoughts, but it is the actions that define them.

Furthermore, there is the aspect of sex. As in *Fanny Hill*, Fielding's basic idea is that "[m]ale power [ ] derives from the phallus; female power, from female beauty and the female capacity for trickery"[41]. Yet, we have to add that in Blifil, it is trickery which makes his power apparent. Tom Jones is the man who lives from his lovers, using the art of making love as a means for surviving in society. But for the female characters, this idea works, as Sophia is beautiful and Lady Bellaston a master (or mistress) of intrigue. Sex does not play a role in Austen's novels. Her characters are interested in being understood, respected and loved. They do not fantasize about sexual relationships in their thoughts, nor do they utter such desires in public. In Fielding's novel, naked bodies and intercourse with changing partners are quite normal. Women run after men, men choose the most beautiful or sexually most attractive and active one - an easy choice as apparently all women who have once had sex are insatiably aroused.

What both authors have in common is the demonstration of the class-system of their time which, in both cases, is defined by distinctions. In Austen's case, marriage is used to introduce differences in rank; in Fielding's it is the consequences of sexual relationships that make the difference. While the poor stay poor (Molly Seagrim is

---

[39] Harrison, Bernard, *Henry Fielding's Tom Jones. The Novelist as Moral Philosopher*, London: 1975, 48.
[40] Harrison, Bernard, *Henry Fielding's Tom Jones. The Novelist as Moral Philosopher*, London: 1975, 48.
"Authorial presence does prevent the building of an illusion of reality: of the facts speaking for themselves. And an interest in the coherence or incoherence of the `public´ surface of a man's discourse and action as we ironically vary the imaginative viewpoint from which we regard it does in Fielding almost wholly drive out any interest in the causal coherence of action and inner life, as in Jane Austen it does not (Jane Austen's authorial presence is far subtler and less intrusive than Fielding's and her irony less bludgeoning, though as accurate: but then her aims are different)."
[41] Spacks, Patricia Meyer, *Desire and Truth*, Chicago: 1990, 56.

pregnant and punished for the fact), the rich can do as they please[42].

Fielding does not offer explanations for his characters' actions because he wants to put his finger on amoral behaviour alone. He does not desire his characters to appear real. It is his exaggerations which produce the effects. Sophia's running away can be called an unsuitable behaviour for a young girl of her time; yet it shows her panic to get away from home and her will to get to Tom. Lady Bellaston's intrigues would have been acceptable, had she not taken to such evil means as rape. These exaggerations - like fables - make very clear that such behaviour is morally incorrect.

In Jane Austen's novels, the reader is confronted with "psychological ralism"[43]. Her characters do not act extraordinarily, but it is their minor gestures and remarks which are reflected upon and explained. Social reality appears more or less the same as in Fielding's days. Where a Molly Seagrim amused herself with changing partners, became pregnant and was punished by society, a protégée called Eliza runs off with a man, becomes pregnant and disappears to a hidden place in the country where she will have to stay unseen by society. One can say, that it is not the facts that have changed in the fifty years between the novels - but Austen as a female writer does not focus on the immoral conduct leading to pregnancy, but on the man's lack of responsibility and on the woman's fate resulting from it. Fielding concentrates on moral. To him, a sinner is a sinner and has to be punished. He has no mercy on human failures, but he ridicules and critisizes them from the viewpoint of his omniscient narrator[44]. His point of view appears hard and cruel because he leaves no room for a personal opinion. His way of presenting the facts imposes his -hypocritically assumed as the right- opinion on his readership. Jane Austen feels with her characters and does not judge them. She provides her readership with the facts leaving all judgment to them[45].

---

[42] Reilly, Patrick, *Tom Jones. Adventure and Providence,* Boston: 1991, 41. Fielding shows the injustices of his society, but he "is no revolutionary - it is a moral, individual reformation that he proposes, not a political and collective restructuring".
[43] Harrison, Bernard, *Henry Fielding's Tom Jones. The Novelist as Moral Philosopher*, London: 1975, 48.
[44] ibd., 45. "Fielding is boisterously present in *Tom Jones.*"
[45] ibd., 46-47.

Literature

Primary Texts

Austen, Jane, *Northanger Abbey*, London: Penguin, 1995.

Austen, Jane, *Sense and Sensibility*, London: Penguin, 1994.

Fielding, Henry, *Tom Jones*, London: Penguin, 1985.

Secondary Texts

Belsey, Catherine, *Desire. Love Stories in Western Culture*, Oxford:
    Blackwell, 1994.

Castellanos, Gabriela, *Laughter, War and Feminism. Elements of Carnival in Three of
    Jane Austen's Novels*, New York: Peter Lang Publishing, 1994.

Grey, David (ed.), *The Jane Austen Handbook*, London: Athlone Press, 1986

Hafner, Dieter, *Tom Jones. Fieldings Roman und Osbornes Drehbuch. Untersuchungen
    zu einem Medienwechsel*, Bern: Francke Verlag, 1981.

Harrison, Bernard, *Henry Fielding's Tom Jones. The Novelist as Moral Philosopher*,
    London: SUP, 1975.

Pease, Allan and Barbara, *Warum Männer nicht zuhören und Frauen schlecht
    einparken. Ganz natürliche Erklärungen für eigentlich unerklärliche
    Schwächen*, München: Ullstein, 2001.

Perkins, Morland, *Reshaping the Sexes in Sense and Sensibility*, Charlottesville,
    London: University Press of Virginia, 1998.

Reilly, Patrick, *Tom Jones. Adventure and Providence*, Boston: Twayne Publishers,
    1991.

Spacks, Patricia Meyer, *Desire and Truth*, Chicago: The University of Chicago Press,
    1990.

Lightning Source UK Ltd.
Milton Keynes UK
UKHW011011150421
382040UK00002B/360

9 783640 318087